Strange Sports with Weird Gear

by Benjamin Lazarus

Editorial Offices: Glenview, Illinois • Parsippany, New Jersey • New York, New York
Sales Offices: Needham, Massachusetts • Duluth, Georgia • Glenview, Illinois
Coppell, Texas • Ontario, California • Mesa, Arizona

Every effort has been made to secure permission and provide appropriate credit for photographic material. The publisher deeply regrets any omission and pledges to correct errors called to its attention in subsequent editions.

Unless otherwise acknowledged, all photographs are the property of Scott Foresman, a division of Pearson Education.

Photo locators denoted as follows: Top (T), Center (C), Bottom (B), Left (L), Right (R), Background (Bkgd)

Cover ©Shaun Best/Reuters/Corbis; 1 ©Reuters/Corbis; 3 ©Reuters/Corbis; 4 ©Layne Kennedy/Corbis; 6 ©Reuters/Corbis; 9 ©Shaun Best/Reuters/Corbis; 10 ©Hulton-Deutsch Collection/Corbis; 12 ©PAUL HANNA/Reuters/Corbis; 15 ©Reuters/Corbis; 17 ©Ray Stubblebine/Reuters/Corbis; 19 ©Scott Halleran /Allsport/Getty Images; 20 ©Owen Franken/Corbis; 22 ©Omar Torres/AFP/Getty Images; 23 ©Getty Images

ISBN: 0-328-13560-7

4 5 6 7 8 9 10 V0G1 14 13 12 11 10 09 08 07 06

Strange Sports Gear

Do you have a favorite sport? Most people can name a sport they most like to play, watch, or both. Everyone knows the most familiar sports in the United States—football, basketball, hockey, and the game that is called our national pastime, baseball. Each of these athletic activities has millions of fans. Yet there are other popular sports that many Americans don't know much about.

Can you imagine playing a sport on **bluish** ice using a stone and brooms? What if you had to wear two different kinds of shoes? Have you heard of a sport that uses wooden baskets? These are some examples of real sports gear. In this book, we will learn about the sports that require some unusual gear. You will read about curling, rhythmic gymnastics, and jai alai.

Each heavy stone is made of granite.

Curling

Curling is a sport that has been played for at least five hundred years. It is played with a heavy polished stone and a specially prepared sheet of ice. The origin of curling is unknown. Some people believe it began in Scotland and others say it started somewhere else in Europe.

Most people think curling has to do with weight-lifting. It's actually a game played on a sheet of ice. It's a little like bowling on ice. Curling describes how the stones naturally curve as they slide across the ice.

Curling is played by two teams of four people. Each player slides two stones. After a stone has been cast by one team, the other team takes a turn. Each team tries to get their stone closest to the goal. Players often try to keep the other team from scoring by knocking that team's stone away from the target.

Why Brooms?

Brooms are an important part of curling. The team captain uses the broom to help the slider aim for the goal. The captain holds the broom next to the goal so that the other player can better aim toward the goal.

Brooms also improve the player's aim by smoothing the ice. One or two people on the same team can sweep the ice in front of the sliding stone. The brooms polish the ice, giving the stone a smoother ride. This also helps the stone to go farther and change direction.

Sweepers must be in good shape; sweeping demands a lot of energy. Curlers must be physically fit. Each curler walks an average of two miles during a game.

Curlers use their brooms to help them aim for the goal.

Different Shoes on the Same Pair of Feet?

Players usually slide on the ice until they let go of the stone. In the early days, it was hard for players to keep their balance. Two different shoes became an important part of the curler's gear. The shoes look like normal sneakers, but there are important differences. One shoe is made to slide easily. The other grips the ice to keep the player from slipping or falling.

Other important rules of the sport are: Each player slides two stones. After a stone has been cast by one of the teams, the other team takes a turn. The player must release the stone twenty-one feet from his team's end, which is called the hogline. Players may try to keep the other team from scoring by knocking a stone already cast by the other team away from the target.

Curlers wear special shoes to help them grip the ice.

Curling: Then and Now

Hundreds of years ago, curling stones weighed as much as 130 pounds. The stones were called boulders. They were so hard to move around that players **skidded** them toward the goal with their feet.

Through the years, the stone has been crafted to curve or curl down the sheet of ice for better aim. The stones now have handles for better control. The stones also have curved bottoms, making them much lighter. Today they weigh only forty-two pounds.

Curling is a sport that is always changing and improving. The methods used to slide the stone and knock out opponents' stones have recently been changed for the better. The quality of curling equipment and the ice sheet have improved as well.

Early curling stones were much heavier than they are today.

Rhythmic Gymnastics

Rhythmic **gymnastics** is not like gymnastics you may be used to seeing. It's gymnastics without **somersaults** or **cartwheels.** Like regular gymnastics, it tests an athlete's strength, balance, and grace. Gymnasts must train carefully or they may end up **wincing** from **throbbing** muscle injuries.

Rhythmic gymnastics combines dancing with gymnastic skills. The routines are performed to music. Athletes add to the beauty of their dancing by using hoops, ropes, balls, ribbons, and clubs.

Rhythmic gymnastics was born in the early 1900s as a combination of exercise programs developed in Europe in the 1800s. A Swedish fitness expert created a kind of gymnastic exercise that concentrated on beautiful movement. At around the same time, an American woman named Catherine Beecher came up with a system of short but physically tough exercises performed to music.

Then, in Switzerland, Emile Dalcroze developed an exercise program for dancers. Finally, George Demeny, a Frenchman, designed exercises performed to music that were meant to improve gracefulness, muscle strength, and posture.

Rhythmic gymnasts are strong and graceful.

Rhythmic Gymnastics Gear

Here's some information about the equipment used in rhythmic gymnastics. The rope is measured to be the same length as the height of the gymnast. It has a knot at each end and can be any color. The rope may be loose or tight when it is moved. It often is made to look like a snake attacking the gymnast, appearing to grab and wrap around the gymnast.

Gymnasts use hoops to spin, roll, and walk through. The hoops are made of wood or plastic that doesn't bend. They are less than three feet across and weigh just over half a pound.

The gymnasts use balls to throw and catch. This is hard to do when a gymnast is always moving! The balls are light and made of rubber or plastic.

Gymnasts often use hoops in their routines.

Clubs are also used in competitions. They are shaped like bottles and are made of wood or plastic. They come in many colors. They weigh at least five ounces and are rolled, twisted, and thrown. They are good pieces of equipment for people who can use both hands equally well, because they need to be handled with care and accuracy.

Ribbons used by rhythmic gymnasts are smooth and silky. They flow through the air gracefully.

Ribbons add to the beauty of the sport.

These ribbons are made of a smooth manmade fabric that feels like silk. They are often attached to a stick made of wood, plastic, or fiberglass. The stick can be painted any color. Ribbons are at least twenty feet long and between 1.5 and 2.5 inches wide. Each ribbon can be one or a combination of colors. Ribbons are thrown in every direction. Gymnasts use them to make designs in the air.

Rhythmic Gymnastics in the Olympics

Rhythmic gymnastics became an Olympic event in 1984. That year, Canadian Lori Fung won the gold medal. It was her moment to shine in the **limelight.**

Gymnasts perform on a forty-foot mat. Each movement they make is judged on how difficult it is and how well it is done. The difficulty level of each movement is written down in a rule book. This rule book also tells judges what a movement should look like if it is done perfectly.

A perfect routine is flawless and performed without **hesitation.** It blends balance and motion. Points are given for grace and flexibility. Each gymnast must keep the gear moving during the whole routine.

Lori Fung won the gold medal in 1984.

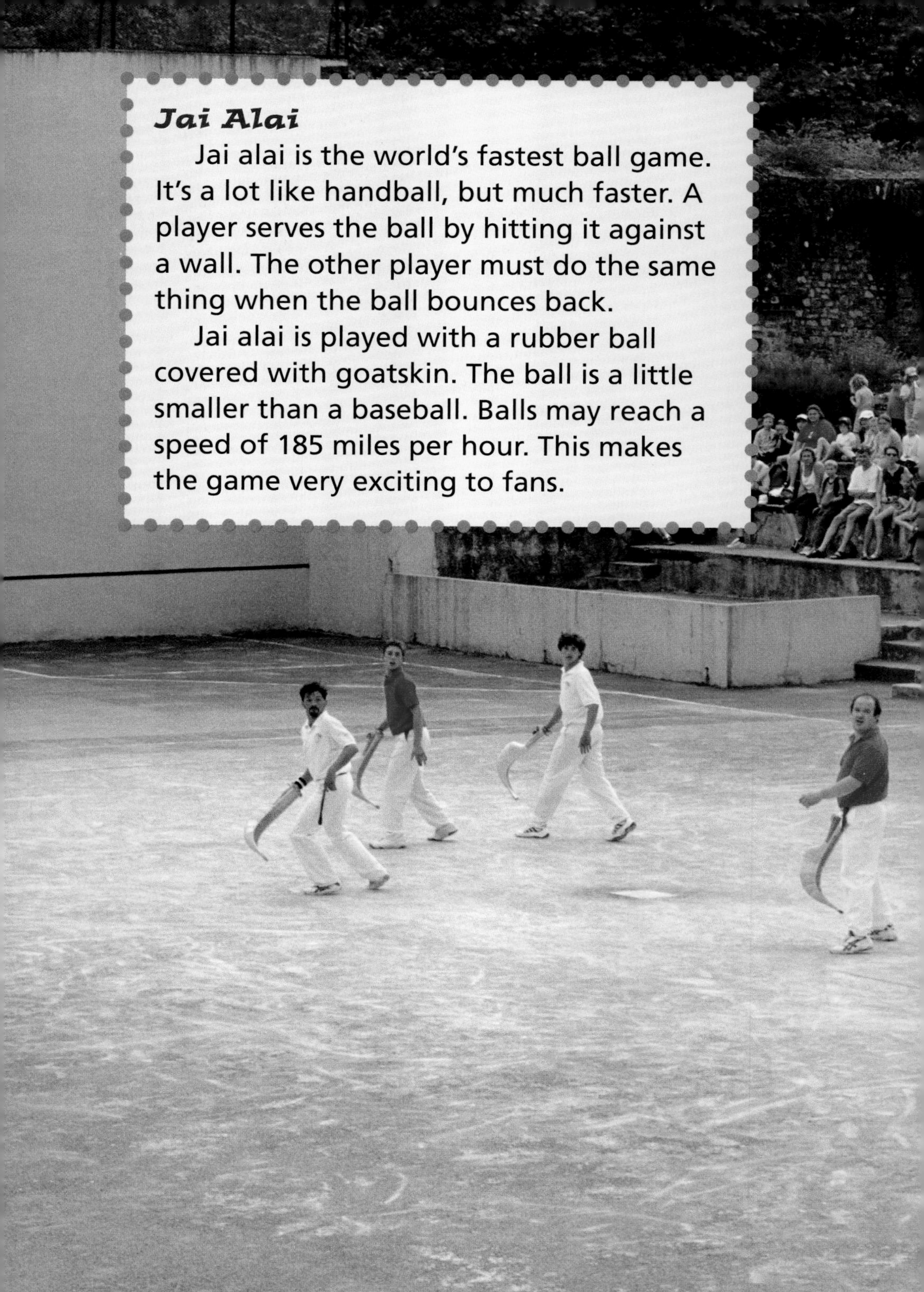

Jai Alai

Jai alai is the world's fastest ball game. It's a lot like handball, but much faster. A player serves the ball by hitting it against a wall. The other player must do the same thing when the ball bounces back.

Jai alai is played with a rubber ball covered with goatskin. The ball is a little smaller than a baseball. Balls may reach a speed of 185 miles per hour. This makes the game very exciting to fans.

How Is Jai Alai Played?

There are four players on each team. Each player lines up, one behind the other. The goal is to throw the ball so fast that the other player can't return it after one bounce. Players are not allowed to block the other team from catching or throwing the ball. The ball must be thrown right after it is caught. It is a fast and difficult game.

Jai Alai Gear

A player uses a wooden basket to catch and throw. Each basket is made to fit a player's hand. It is covered with a leather glove. The ball travels so fast that the players have to wear helmets.

The playing wall has to be strong to withstand such a powerful game. The wall is made of thick granite blocks eighteen inches thick.

Glossary

bluish *adj.* bluelike in color.

cartwheels *n.* sideways handsprings.

gymnastics *n.* exercises that use strength, agility, coordination, and balance.

hesitation *n.* a pause or doubt.

limelight *n.* the focus of attention.

skidded *v.* slid while moving.

somersaults *n.* stunts performed by turning heels over head.

throbbing *v.* pulsing or aching.

wincing *v.* shrinking away; flinching slightly.